SAFETY TOWN ®

When I Cross the Street

By Dorothy Chlad

Illustrations by Lydia Halverson

CHILDRENS PRESS ®

CHICAGO

Library of Congress Cataloging in Publication Data

Chlad, Dorothy.
  When I cross the street

  (Safety Town)
  Summary: Presents general safety rules to
be followed when crossing streets in the city
and in the country.
    1.   Traffic safety—Juvenile literature.
[1.   Traffic safety.   2.   Safety]   I.   Halverson,
Lydia, ill.   II.   Title.   III.   Series: Chlad,
Dorothy. Safety Town.
HE5614.C52   363.1'2575'088054   81-18099
ISBN 0-516-01985-6   AACR2

Hi . . . my name is Mary.

I want to help
you cross the street
safely. I am going
to show and tell you
my safety rules.

This is what I do.

I always stop at
the curb.

Then I look ... left ...

right ...

left.

I watch for turning cars.

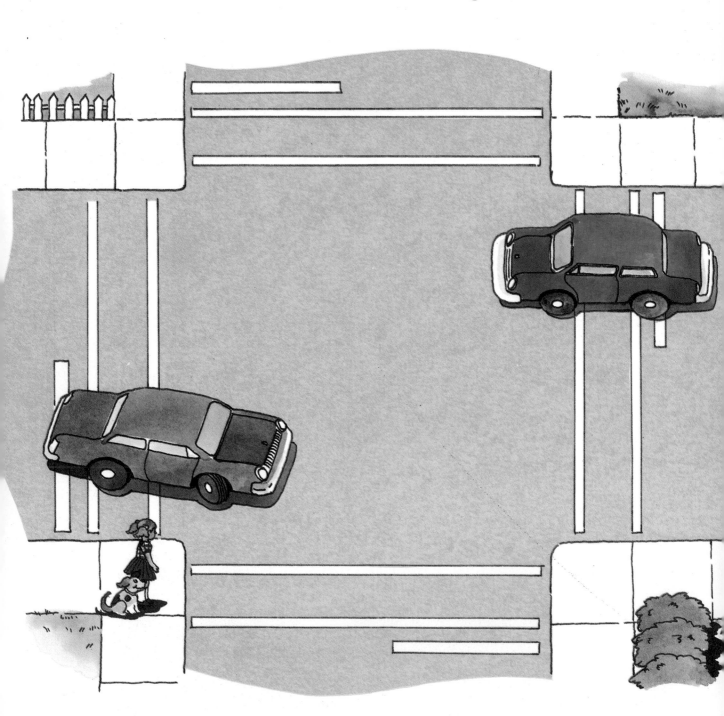

I always listen for sirens.

Police cars,
fire trucks, and
ambulances have
sirens. When you hear
a siren, stop at the curb.
The siren tells you
the cars are in a hurry
to help people.

At a traffic light I wait
for the green light.

I always wait for the
walk lights.

I always make sure
that drivers can see
my eyes before
I cross the street.

I always remember
my safety rules.

Stop at the curb.
Look left.
Look right.
Look left.
Watch for turning cars.
Listen for sirens.

When it rains or snows I am very careful.

Rain and snow make the streets and sidewalks slippery.

I always wear my
raincoat and boots
in the rain.

I always wear my
big coat and big
boots in the snow.

Sometimes I visit
my friend José.

He lives in a city
with big buildings.

We always stop
at the driveways.
We always watch
for cars and trucks.

We are always
very careful.
We want to get
to the playground
safely.

I walk to school
with my friends.
   We always stop
at the driveways
and look for cars
and trucks.

At some cross
walks the
guard helps us
cross the street.

Sometimes I visit
my friend Ann.

She lives in the country.

We are careful when
we cross the road.

We look for cars,
trucks, buses,
motorcycles, and
tractors.

At night we wear bright, shiny clothes. Now the drivers can see us better.

Please remember
my safety rules when
you cross the street.

Stop at the curb.
Look left.
Look right.
Look left.
Watch for turning cars.
Listen for sirens.

About the Author

Dorothy Chlad, founder of the total concept of Safety Town, is recognized internationally as a leader in Preschool/Early Childhood Safety Education. She has authored eight books on the program, and has conducted the only workshops dedicated to the concept. Under Mrs. Chlad's direction, the National Safety Town Center was founded to promote the program through community involvement.

She has presented the importance of safety education at local, state, and national safety and education conferences, such as National Community Education Association, National Safety Council, and the American Driver and Traffic Safety Education Association. She serves as a member of several national committees, such as the Highway Traffic Safety Division and the Educational Resources Division of National Safety Council. Chlad was an active participant at the Sixth International Conference on Safety Education.

Dorothy Chlad continues to serve as a consultant for State Departments of Safety and Education. She has also consulted for the TV program "Sesame Street" and recently wrote this series of safety books for Childrens Press.

A participant of White House Conferences on safety, Dorothy Chlad has received numerous honors and awards including National Volunteer Activist and YMCA Career Woman of Achievement.

About the Artist

Lydia Halverson was born Lydia Geretti in midtown Manhattan. When she was two, her parents left New York and moved to Italy. Four years later her family returned to the United States and settled in the Chicago Area. Lydia attended the University of Illinois, graduating with a degree in fine arts. She worked as a graphic designer for many years before finally concentrating on book illustration.

Lydia lives with her husband and two cats in a suburb of Chicago and is active in several environmental organizations.